Talking Heads:

Your Guide to Finding a Qualified Therapist in the UK

Talking Heads:

Your Guide to Finding a Qualified Therapist in the UK

By Dr Tara Quinn-Cirillo &
Dr Marianne Trent

Talking Heads:
Your Guide to Finding a Qualified Therapist in the UK

First published in the UK by KDP, 2023.
Copyright © Dr Tara Quinn-Cirillo, Dr Marianne Trent, 2023.
All rights reserved.
ISBN: 9798871161050
Imprint: Independently published.

Also available in e-book.

Created and compiled: Dr Tara Quinn-Cirillo and Dr Marianne Trent.
Indexed and edited: Dr Tara Quinn-Cirillo and Dr Marianne Trent.
Proofread: Christabel Fitch and Francis Quinn
Cover & Book Design: Dr Marianne Trent
Author Photographs: Dr Marianne Trent and Dr Tara Quinn-Cirillo

About the Authors

Dr Tara Quinn-Cirillo, CPsychol AFBPsS DCounsPsych, PPDip, MSc, BSc (Hons), HCPC Registered Counselling Psychologist.

Dr Tara Quinn-Cirillo is a HCPC Registered Counselling Psychologist. She also a Chartered Psychologist with The British Psychological Society and holds Associate Fellow (AFBPsS) status. She has over 20 years clinical experience in mental health, neurodivergence, disability and human behaviour.

Tara is the Founder and Director of The Conversation Starter Project CIC which is a grassroots Community Wellbeing Project tackling loneliness, emotional health and physical wellbeing in Sussex. She also has a particular interest in supporting the voluntary sector through this work.

Tara is an accomplished broadcaster and media expert globally and the host of The Adversity Psychologist Podcast. She has a keen interest in the ethics of mental health provision and regulation of mental health psychologists including the dissemination of information via the media and social media. She has been involved in many innovative collaborations with health and wellbeing platforms with the aim of bringing good quality mental health knowledge to the public.

Dr Quinn-Cirillo worked in the NHS for 15 years before setting up her own private practice in Sussex. Her extraneous roles include Specialist Advisor for the CQC, Clinical Reviewer for NHS England and Volunteer for the British Red Cross.

Find out more at **www.drtara.co.uk**

Dr Marianne Trent, DclinPsy CPsychol PGCert BSc (Hons), HCPC Registered Clinical Psychologist.

Dr Marianne Trent is a Clinical Psychologist in Private Practice. She specialises in Trauma, Grief, Anxiety and Depression. She also supports the needs of Aspiring Psychologists.

This is Marianne's fourth book, with her others including *The Grief Collective: Stories of Life, Loss & Learning to Heal, The Clinical Psychologist Collective: Advice & Guidance for Aspiring Clinical Psychologists* and *The Aspiring Psychologist Collective: Reflective Accounts of Mental Health Professionals on their way to Qualification.*

Dr Trent is a media regular, writing about mental health related topics and concepts. She has been interviewed live on BBC News and has written for the British Psychological Society's magazine The Psychologist, The Guardian, Psychologies, Platinum Magazine, Huff Post, The Telegraph and more. She was also featured in Channel 5's *Inheritance Wars: Who Gets the Money?* She is also the host of The Aspiring Psychologist Podcast which launched in December 2021.

Last but never least, Marianne is an ambassador for AtALoss.org and a Clinical Advisor for 'Our Time', a charity that support young adults who have experienced parental loss.

Website:	www.goodthinkingpsychology.co.uk
Instagram:	@DrMarianneTrent
Facebook:	Dr Marianne Trent
YouTube:	Dr Marianne Trent
LinkedIn:	Dr Marianne Trent
TikTok:	@drmariannetrent
Twitter:	@DrMarianneTrent

Dedication

This booklet is to you and to everyone else who either wants to enable themselves to feel better or to help support someone else to feel better. It is also for all the hardworking, dedicated and qualified clinicians out there making the world a better place.

Thank you,
Tara and Marianne.

Disclaimer

This guidance refers to sourcing talking therapy by individuals practicing in the UK.

This is a guide and not definitive advice. Please ensure you check the qualifications and regulation details of anyone you are considering seeing for therapy.

This booklet is intended for informational purposes only and does not constitute legal advice or a guarantee of safe clinical practice from any chosen therapist. While every effort has been made to ensure the accuracy and reliability of the information provided, it is important to note that the facts presented in this booklet have not been independently verified by a legal team.

The information we will introduce you to over these next pages will refer to sourcing therapists in an independent/private practice setting. It doesn't include practitioners within the NHS (National Health Service), or other public sector organisations. However, it might well be useful to you as you try to understand what the skills, expertise and experience of people you might meet in public sector services, actually means.

The author and publisher make no representations or warranties regarding the completeness, accuracy, or applicability of the information contained herein. The use of information presented in this booklet is at the reader's own risk, and the author and publisher shall not be liable for any direct, indirect, incidental, consequential, or punitive damages arising out of the use or reliance on the information contained herein.

The authors have approached organisations for their consent to include their logos. Should you be reading this and wish for your logo to be removed please contact the authors and this will be redressed at the earliest opportunity. Any use of logos in this booklet does not mean we are in any way affiliated by the organisations being discussed.

This disclaimer applies to all content within the booklet, including but not limited to text, graphics, images, and any other material. By reading this booklet, you acknowledge and agree to the terms of this disclaimer. If you do not agree with these terms, it is recommended that you seek professional advice before relying on any information presented in this publication. If in doubt and still feeling a bit lost, a chat with your GP is often a great place to start.

Contents

PART 1:

Why it Matters

Background to this book

There have been a number of documented cases where people have offered talking therapy when they are not suitably qualified to do so. In such cases this means they are unqualified, unregulated and even uninsured. They might also make massively inflated claims about the results people can expect by working with them. They may even try using titles which suggest they are more qualified than they are. This might include using the terms therapist, psychologist, psychotherapist and counsellor. However, in order to ethically use these titles, people should have the relevant training, qualifications, experience and supervision.

Over the last few years as many of our lives have shifted in a more online direction, we might also have found we've been bombarded with adverts for unsuitably qualified therapists. You might have spotted them in your social media feeds, as sponsored posts in your search engine or via your browser home page. With this in mind, when actually trying to find a therapist, it can feel a bit like navigating a minefield without a map. We decided that via this booklet we'd love to be your trusted, expert guides. We'll help you get to where you want to go and where you'd like to be by dodging the pitfalls and hotspots. We will be laying out some pointers for what questions to ask and what qualifications to expect as the norm when finding a suitably qualified and regulated therapist, counsellor, psychotherapist or psychologist.

You may have seen stories in the media about members of the public who have fallen victim to unqualified and unregulated therapists.

You deserve to feel as calm, happy, and as distress free as possible and over the years many have got better at talking loud and proud about their own mental health and their right to do so. As a result, even in the years prior to the Coronavirus Pandemic, mental health and its treatment was starting to get more of the attention it deserved and, as a result, the NHS and private services were already creaking a little under the increased demand. From 2020 – 2024 there were a couple of lockdowns, some very scary times, mixed in with energy poverty, the cost of living crisis, isolation and uncertainty, the impact upon emotional health has, of course, been huge. As a result, therapists in the UK offering talking therapy for emotional health issues have experienced a huge increase in demand for their services. It also means new 'therapists' have appeared to plug the gaps. Some more ethical and qualified than others. T

In this booklet, we will be talking about people who are offering a therapeutic service to the public for anxiety or depression. In essence, they are offering a clinical service and need to be appropriately qualified and registered. The function of this is so that they can be monitored and held accountable, and that they continue to engage in professional development; accessing the right kind of clinical supervision and implementing a robust, ethical framework. It is important that we help educate the public on this issue as there will always be some individuals who operate outside of this framework. The framework is there to keep the public safe, and to keep practitioners accountable. That is what makes a good and ethical practitioner. It is not always clear to the public what the pathways are to ensure that they are able to source an appropriately qualified and regulated practitioner.

When we were preparing to finalise this booklet, we received the following message, which highlights our 'why' for this booklet.

Hi Tara.
I hope you don't mind the message. I came across a post of yours about unregulated psychologists and I'm trying to find out if there are any groups advocating for this to stop. I have past experience of being 'treated' by a psychologist who turned out to only have a BSc in psychology, and not registered. Myself and others who were also unethically treated by this person want to do anything we can to ensure this can't happen to others. Are there any groups you might be able to signpost me to, or are you aware of anything I could get involved with? Thanks so much, Kiri.

Well, we don't have a group to direct people to, not yet anyway, but let's see how this guide is received! We hope this booklet creates some useful discussions and that it helps people to make sense of what qualified and regulated professionals are and why it matters. We care passionately about easing people's distress in safe and effective ways.

Modern times and modern methods

Both NHS and private services continue to face ongoing demand. This means that more and more people are seeking talking therapy options outside the NHS. The digital age is also a considerable factor as the public can access support in ways never previously possible. This now means that options for accessing services includes:

— Digital mental health platforms,
— Telephone therapy,
— Text message therapy,
— Online video therapy,
— Online group services / programmes;
— & more!

Unfortunately, in response to the increased demand and also to make a living, sometimes people have started offering unqualified and sometimes dangerous 'therapy'. Even some who might mean well, but not appropriately qualified or experienced are often not suitable to be offering talking therapy to the public. The move to online communication and therapy has meant that members of the public can be vulnerable to adverts from unqualified and regulated therapists. They might crop up in social media timelines and in some cases in social media groups either as adverts or expert commentary. A number of documentaries have highlighted heart-breaking narratives of those who have been mistreated by unqualified and unregulated therapists or in some cases companies offering seemingly 'magical' solutions to presenting conditions such as depression and anxiety often at greatly exaggerated cost to the individual. This kind of unscrupulous and unethical practice is sadly becoming commonplace in today's world. However, please don't worry. There are also countless examples of excellent and appropriately qualified professionals and by following our advice in this booklet you will dramatically increase your chances of finding them!

Why do ethics matter?

Sometimes people using the term therapist, psychologist, psychotherapist, or counsellor, might not have the training or credentials you'd want them to in order to be advertising themselves as such.

When people say something untrue about their professional skills and experiences it is considered unethical. That means it is unfair, inappropriate and might well have been used as an attempt to mislead and to charge money for a service.

When reading and hearing the stories about unethical practitioners either from stories in the media or from clients of such practitioners who have shared their story with us personally, we are struck by not only the numbers of unregulated and unqualified practitioners but the level of unethical practice. Examples include asking patients to video themselves doing specific therapy strategies to be then shared on social media, sharing details of other patients, and making derogatory comments about them, appearing overtly disinterested in the person's experiences of and within 'therapy' sessions to name just a few.

Entering into an appropriately qualified and regulated professional therapy means you should feel safe and in control, never exploited or uncomfortable with the way you are being spoken about or to either in person or away from sessions.

With these issues in mind, for those wishing to find a therapist it can, therefore, be a minefield. There is a wealth of advice out there on mental health and wellbeing. It can also be tricky to work out when the next level of intervention is required. This might mean moving beyond general wellbeing hubs, apps and online advice. Sometimes it may mean a need to access more formal support for your emotional health such as a therapist, counsellor or psychologist. But how do you begin to find someone suitable?

It can look like we as authors here are being very protective over what we do as qualified and regulated psychologists. But for us, it is about safety; protecting the public and helping them make informed choices about the services they receive. For example, if you are anxious or depressed, how may this impact your ability to really look into someone and the credentials they offer? There is a huge trust element here and that's why it is really important that we speak out and try and help people make some choices about who they see.

Producing this booklet is the most appropriate way we could think of to really be ethical and to help you to make informed choices about your care and treatment.

Possible "red flags"

These are some of the factors we personally and professionally consider a bit suspect which might indicate a potential red flag about a clinician or service.

- Discounts/sign up schemes
- Practitioners not providing you with registration numbers or being open about regulation and looking them up.
- Offering a 'discount' on sessions for leaving a review or doing a video for social media.
- Asking you to make videos for social media or advertising.
- Asking you to join WhatsApp groups with other patients.

If it feels wrong.....don't ignore that!

Surely, I am safe if they call themselves a psychologist?

The term 'psychologist' alone is not a protected title. Anyone can use this! Yes, it is true! Unfortunately, it's more of that unethical behaviour we mentioned earlier.

When you see someone calling themselves a psychologist, you would naturally assume someone is a qualified psychologist. As members of the public, you have the right to know if someone using this title is a qualified psychologist or someone with 'just' a 3-year undergraduate degree in psychology but have not gone on to complete formal training and qualifications in applied psychology. Even as you read this you might think 'well, they have a degree in psychology.... Sounds good enough, surely?' The majority of UK based Psychology degrees do not offer skills

8

or practice in counselling or therapy. They are theory-based courses which introduce concepts and theories but *do not* cover any clinical skills in actually delivering therapy or treatment. This is the essential aspect for anyone offering a mental health service to the public. An ethical practitioner will be open about their training and qualifications and show you how to go and look them up on their respective register. If they are not, then this can be considered a huge red flag.

Surely, I am safe if they call themselves a therapist?

It may also come as a surprise that even the term 'therapist' is not protected. This means anyone who wants to can legally call themselves a therapist. They do not need to have any formal qualifications or even have seen or helped any clients at all. We would hope that the vast majority of people using a therapist title are appropriately skilled and qualified, but we wanted to flag this with you so that you are aware as you set about your research.

Safety

A safety issue with unregulated and unqualified psychologists and therapists is that they can be providing services to the public that they are simply not qualified to be offering. This presents a risk. In current times the treatment approaches are varied: online, face to face, digital mental health platforms, WhatsApp groups, social media groups and more. There is, therefore, a huge potential for risk when an unqualified practitioner is providing mental health input. We need to think about what happens if a risk situation related to a client gets missed because the practitioner doesn't have the training to assess or they don't have the ability to think about how they would conduct a risk assessment. Keeping the public safe as well as supporting them with their difficulties is what differentiates ethical, qualified and regulated practitioners. The safety issues we are talking about means that if their mental health care and treatment is not appropriate then they might pose a risk to themselves, their family or the general public.

Qualifications and Regulation for Therapists

When it comes to talking therapy in the UK, you might have heard of the terms 'appropriately qualified' and 'regulated'. It is important that we run through what these terms mean as they are vital for sourcing a therapist.

Appropriately Qualified – This means that individual holds the correct academic qualifications to provide the service they are offering and use the title they are advertising. This consists of a professional training course with an established training institution/awarding body.

Regulated - It is important to understand what professional regulation is and how to check if someone is regulated. You are advised to check that the individual is registered with the professional body for the service they are offering. You may ask why regulatory bodies are important if someone is 'qualified'. Well, the purpose of these regulatory bodies is to provide a framework for practice standards including qualifications, supervision, indemnity insurance and clinical governance with the aim to protect the public from harm. Being regulated means the individual is accountable to a public body who monitor ethical and robust practice. When someone is regulated, it means if you experience a problem with the service, you have received that you can make a complaint to the regulator. This will then be investigated to see if there are any fitness to practice issues. If someone is not regulated, then you have no ability to complain or raise concerns in a way which will be followed up on to safeguard you and others.

The reason we want to educate others about the importance of qualifications and regulation for talking therapy, is summarised well in the following illustration: if an unqualified doctor carried out a medical procedure, then this would be dealt with by law. Yet if an unqualified/unregulated therapist inappropriately treats someone's fragile mental health then it is quite astounding there is still no legal framework for dealing with this. However, when a health professional is qualified and regulated there can be an appropriate investigation made to explore any issues around their practice and to safeguard the public in future if required.

In this booklet, we are talking about people who are offering a therapeutic service to the public for things such as anxiety or depression. In essence, they are offering a clinical service and they should be appropriately qualified and registered. The function of this is so that they can be monitored and held accountable and continue to engage in professional development and operate using a robust ethical framework. It is important that we help educate the public on this issue as there will always be some individuals who operate outside of this framework. The framework is there to keep the public safe and to keep practitioners accountable. That is what makes a good ethical practitioner. It is not always clear to the public what the pathways are to ensure that they are able to source an appropriately qualified and regulated practitioner.

Types of Required Regulation

Psychologists offering a clinical service to the public - adults and children

The Health and Care Professions Council (HCPC) are the regulatory body for qualified psychologists and a wide range of other professions such as paramedics, radiologists, dieticians and more. There are 9 psychologist titles covered by the HCPC and protected by law. Anyone who uses these titles MUST be on the HCPC register.

These job titles are:

- Practitioner Psychologist
- Registered Psychologist
- Clinical Psychologist
- Counselling Psychologist
- Forensic Psychologist
- Health Psychologist
- Educational Psychologist
- Occupational Psychologist
- Sports and Exercise Psychologist

As explained above, a psychologist offering a service to the public MUST be registered with the HCPC as above. This makes it easier because you can look then look them up on the HCPC website. For transparency, for example, you will find both of us on there[12] because we are qualified and regulated. So, if anybody says they are a qualified 'psychologist' and is offering a service to the public, you WILL be able to look them up on the 'check the register' function[3]. It's free to access and their name will be there. If it's not there, then ask them for more information about why or choose a different therapist.

A Note on Training Overseas

Psychologists who trained overseas must register with the HCPC in the UK in order to satisfy that they meet criteria to practice in the UK. In order to attest that they are appropriately skilled and qualified they might also need to have completed a relevant conversion course with the British Psychological Society, (BPS).

---

[1] https://www.hcpc-uk.org/check-the-register/register-results/?query=quinn-cirillo&profession=PYL
[2] https://www.hcpc-uk.org/check-the-register/register-results/?query=trent&profession=PYL
[3] https://www.hcpc-uk.org/check-the-register/

Coaching Psychologists

Coaching Psychologists are not regulated by the HCPC, and the term 'coaching psychologist' is not a protected title. Technically it would be legally possible for someone to call themselves a coaching psychologist with no professional qualifications. However, it is also possible to be a qualified psychologist with additional skills in coaching and ethically call yourself a coaching psychologist. Yes, told you it was all a little confusing....

Some coaching psychologists choose to seek Accreditation and Chartership through the British Psychological Society. Please refer to The British Psychological Society guidance and register for coaching psychologists and their qualifications and area of work. Remember, it is okay to ask any clinician you are considering working with about their qualifications, registrations, skills and experience.

https://portal.bps.org.uk/Psychologist-Search/Register-of-Coaching-Psychologists

Clinical Associate Psychologists / Psychological Wellbeing Practitioners

When searching for psychologists you may come across the terms Clinical Associate Psychologists (CAP) and Psychological Wellbeing Practitioners (PWP). These are newer psychology roles but are not fully qualified psychologists. You may predominantly find these clinicians working in NHS services but over time you may also see more of them practising in private services too.

These roles are regulated by the British Psychological Society (BPS). They are not regulated by law as in the case of qualified psychologists. Since the 10th of June 2022, NHS England have required that PWPs register either with the BPS or the BABCP (British Association of Behavioural and Cognitive Psychotherapy). They also have to have completed a BPS accredited mental health training programme (APT).

You can learn more about the exact roles, training and ways in which they are allowed to work on the BPS website:

https://www.bps.org.uk/psychological-wellbeing-practitioner-job-profile

https://www.bps.org.uk/clinical-associate-psychology-england-and-clinical-associate-applied-psychology-scotland-job

Research Psychologists

Research psychologists are in a slightly different criteria to those psychologists mentioned above. They might have a Doctorate in Philosophy, also known as a PhD. They may have a doctorate in another area of psychology such as clinical, counselling, forensic or health, for example, and be a chartered member of the British Psychological Society (BPS). If they are offering a therapeutic service to the public, then they need to have completed relevant training to register with the HCPC.

Although research psychologists tend to conduct their research in academic or laboratory style environments, they may also use more clinical settings such as hospitals or patient homes to conduct research. You wouldn't typically expect to find a research / academic psychologist working with the public and offering assessment and treatment services using 'applied psychology'. If they are, we would expect and hope that they have additional practical training and are, therefore, registered with the HCPC.

Other Therapists

There are so many other types of therapists including: Art Therapists, Dialectical Behavioural Therapists (DBT), Psychotherapists, Humanistic Therapist, Counsellor, Cognitive Behavioural Therapists (CBT), Couples Therapists, Addictions Therapist and many more. This is such a case by case, therapist by therapist basis. Someone who is a DBT Therapist usually has to have a core background as a qualified mental health professional such as a qualified psychologist, occupational therapist or mental health nurse. As explained in the earlier section, counselling and psychotherapy are not regulated professions in the UK. This means anyone can say they are a therapist without having the registration or membership of a professional body. Instead, in the UK, there is the Professional Standards Authority (PSA) accredited registers programme. This is a voluntary scheme which accredits those professional bodies which hold a register, so that members of the public can be confident when choosing health and care practitioners. Professional bodies for therapy registered by the PSA include British Association for Behavioural and Cognitive Therapists, (BABCP), UK Council for Psychotherapy, (UKCP), British Psychoanalytic Council, (BPC), National Counselling and Psychotherapy Society, (NCPS) and others.

We advise anyone seeking therapy to check the therapist is currently a member of a professional body that has a PSA accredited register. This means they'll know they're seeing a therapist who's highly qualified and who is committed to high professional and ethical standards. It also means if they want to make a complaint there is a process and support available.

PART 2:

What is therapy?

What is therapy anyway?

What an excellent question! We feel this conundrum hasn't really been helped by the fact that 'the therapist' or 'the psychologist' often turns out to be a bit warped, twisted and sometimes even completely corrupt and illegal in loads of TV series and films. Come on, now writing teams, whilst it makes good drama there's also a fair few seeds of doubt and mistrust you're sowing internationally too which may be contributing to people delaying accessing treatment and could even be costing lives.

So, even taking into account that there's lots of different types of therapy having given it a quick google it seems even the internet is somewhat undecided on what the definition of therapy is exactly so let us freestyle. We see a therapeutic relationship as being one which feels safe, trusted, non-judgmental, informed and helpful. It should be one which makes you feel less alone, less scared, more hopeful, more understood, de-shamed and basically all of the good stuff. That's not to say that accessing talking therapy is a walk in the park or won't bring up some painful emotions but please don't give too much mind to that old, kind of threatening saying that: *"It'll get worse before it gets better...."* Because, when therapy is delivered safely and ethically, we don't believe this to be the case. A safe, therapeutic relationship will be one where you don't feel swamped, overwhelmed or like you're left struggling with negative or painful thoughts, feelings or memories without first having developed the coping methods, distress tolerance techniques and healing strategies to mean that the pain is tolerable or even transformed or neutralised.

So, what happens in therapy?

Generally speaking therapy is two people, yourself and the therapist although of course systemic, family, couples and group work would be an exception to this. A time and date is usually made at mutually convenient times although sometimes in services such as the NHS appointments may just be sent to you in the post without much wiggle room at least initially. The appointments will either be in person, via a video conferencing platform or over the phone. If you're accessing it from home, it's usually important that you be in a quiet room with the door closed and that you feel comfortable speaking openly wherever you are speaking from.

Your therapist will usually conduct an initial assessment with you where they will pull together a picture of what is happening for you, how it is impacting you and a treatment plan to address this. This should be clear to both of you and discussed with you. Therapy should be collaborative - ie it is not something that is "done" to you, rather a process you go through together.

Sometimes clients have told us in the past that they 'almost didn't attend because they were worried, they wouldn't know what to say.' Or that they would 'get it wrong'. Don't worry, this can be a really common fear but please remember that in the majority of therapies the therapist will lead the session and ask you questions which help them to work out what is going on for you, what has led to it happening, what might be keeping it in place and to get an idea of the types of treatments or approaches which might best help you to live a more fulfilling, satisfying life with less distress and more joy.

What sort of things can I get therapy for?

Honestly, the list is almost limitless! Here's some common reasons for people choosing to access therapy:

Depression
Trauma
Military Service
Sexual Assault
Alcohol Use
Eating disorders
Bipolar Disorder
Anxiety
Grief
Abuse
Drink Spiking
Drug use / dependency
Phobias
Birth Trauma
Gender Disappointment
Breastfeeding Trauma
ADHD
Autism
Relationship Issues
Stress Management

Parenting Stress
Coping with Change
Perfectionism
Ageing and life transitions
Chronic Pain
Sleep Problems
Chronic Illness
Death Anxiety
Obsessive Compulsive
Disorder (OCD)
Performance anxiety
Co-dependency
Body Dysmorphia

Some client examples for context

If you're brand new to this it can feel tricky to get your head around what might be involved so let us guide you through a couple of made up cases with what would be a roughly appropriate treatment plan / approach. These cases have been written with a qualified clinical psychologist in mind as the treating clinician[4] but hopefully this will be helpful even if you're not considering working with a therapist of this nature.

Whilst this is a booklet intended for adults, we have included a case study of a young person because we know you may be reading this in order to work out the best way to get qualified therapy for a minor.

---

[4] Sorry, I find it hard to write from another clinician's perspective but I hope you will still find this useful.

Angela

Angela is 78. She lives alone. Her husband died in hospital in May 2020. She has a daughter, son-in-law and 16 year old grandson who all live in Australia. She is a retired nurse. She is struggling with anxiety and depression and says that she feels very lonely. She misses her husband and finds herself imagining his death. Her sleep is broken. Her health is generally good.

Angela's Proposed Therapy

Angela is seen for an initial assessment where she is asked about herself, the things she likes to do, the current sorts of thoughts and feelings she is experiencing and what it seems like her problems are and how they are impacting upon her wellbeing, functioning and risk to self and others. By the end of the first session the psychologist summarises some of the things they have spoken about and says:

"It sounds like you enjoyed a wonderful relationship with your husband and since your son and his family moved away you had built a very enjoyable life with one another and rarely felt bored or lonely. When your husband died it was during the pandemic and due to restrictions, you weren't able to be with him. This was very difficult for you from a personal and also a professional position as you felt you were denied the chance to be there for him as a wife or an ex-nurse. You are experiencing symptoms of trauma imagining what his death must have been like and feeling that your life feels emptier and less purposeful without him. It also makes you feel disloyal when you do have some occasions of enjoyment because you will then suddenly remember that he is dead and yet you are smiling which makes you feel a whole range of complicated and painful emotions. I think it would be really helpful for us to work together so that we can help you to manage the painful thoughts, feelings and memories you're experiencing. I also think it would be helpful for us to help the intrusive thoughts and memories you're having to lay flatter using a technique such as eye movement desensitisation and reprocessing (EMDR). I think that this proposed treatment will mean that you are able to look back on your memories of your husband and your time together with fondness and with pleasure but with less of the really de-railing pain and guilt you're currently experiencing. This in turn will

25

free you up to live your life more mindfully in the present and in future."

Angela's treatment outcomes

Angela is seen for 24 sessions of self-funded therapy. By the time she is discharged she is feeling happier, calmer and more connected to her life right now. She has started volunteering at a local charity shop and enjoys chatting with the locals there. She has also become part of a local choir and likes that there are people there who are older and younger than her and who seem to value her company and her input into the choir. She still thinks of her husband and still misses him and the life they shared together but she is less consumed by her grief for him which she now recognises was not just grief but grief overlaid with trauma and lots of other complicated feelings. Now the trauma has been processed and is not distressing her, she feels she can cope with the grief she is left with. She also knows that in living her life even though her husband is dead that this is not being disloyal to his memory.

Fahra

Fahra is 14. She lives with her parents and 2 older sisters. She is a high achiever, usually finding school pretty easy. During the first lockdown she started trying to watch what she was eating. She was pleased to notice that she had been losing weight. She followed lots of weight loss pages on Instagram and TikTok. She started restricting her eating and exercising daily. Her periods which started when she was 12 have not come for the last 2 months. Fahra and her family are all finding mealtimes very stressful and they are not sure what to do.

Fahra's Proposed Therapy

Like anyone with eating disorders it can be tricky because it's often the case that the ultimate goal of the illness is to be left alone. However, because there is currently a risk to her she agreed to be seen and chose to be seen for half of the assessment with her parents and half by herself. Some of the assessment session is spent on rapport building because this work can feel very intrusive. A history is taken which includes, past, present and hopes for the future. By the end of the initial assessment session the psychologist summarises some of the things they have spoken about and says:

"Your Mum explained that when you were a baby you had a problem with your stomach which meant you needed special medical supervision. This has now been resolved but it meant that at mealtimes you found there was focus on you and people seemed pleased when you ate. Your sisters are 10 and 12 years older than you and you said it felt like you had a slightly different upbringing to them and like they're kind of half-sisters because they led such different lives to you. It sounds like things were going ok for you when the lockdown happened, but you had become very focused on GCSE's being a big deal and needing to do well in order to go on to become a doctor. Shortly before the lockdown someone mentioned you'd put on weight and so the time away from people felt like a golden opportunity to get in shape. Understandably when people began to say how good you looked this felt tricky to give up. Currently your period has stopped, and this is likely because your food intake combined with exercise means that your body doesn't currently have the spare energy to lose via a menstrual period. I'd like you to be seen by your GP for monitoring and blood tests and by our team psychiatrist so that we can check your physical observations and make sure you are as well as possible currently. In terms of the work we will do, family

therapy is an evidence-based approach for people with eating disorders. Alongside this it would be helpful for you to be seen to work towards our agreed goals of increasing your self-compassion, decreasing perfectionism and self-criticism and working through strategies to help you be able to manage the distress caused by difficult thoughts and feelings. The aim is that by the end of our work you'll feel kinder to yourself, and you'll feel able to eat without such strong feelings of guilt, shame and disgust which will then mean you're freed up to do really well in your GCSE's and beyond."

Fahra's treatment outcomes

Fahra is seen for 70 sessions over the next 18 months or so. This is a combination of 1:1 work with a clinical psychologist and of family therapy in which her clinical psychologist is part of the team. By the time she is discharged she is feeling more able to cope and enjoys a more functional relationship with her parents and siblings. She is feeling normal levels of apprehension about her upcoming GCSE's but is able to ask her teachers and friends for guidance if she feels she doesn't understand something. She has learned to tolerate feelings in her body linked to eating and digestion which previously felt very triggering. She is aware of her early warning risk signs which are usually self-critical in nature. She is now well versed in self-compassion and knows it should be a daily practice and that sleeping well and having a good work life balance is essential for good mental and physical health.

Patrick

Patrick is 24. He lives by himself but has a girlfriend. He was recently promoted in his marketing job at the same time as the company moved to new premises. There is now an expectation that he will lead meetings and do presentations. This is previously something he has felt okay about but in the new building the conference room walls are all made of glass and he keeps getting panicked at the idea that he won't cope and that anyone walking past the office will see how red he is and that he is doing an awful job and that he will be sacked and this will be awful for his long term career. He is struggling to go to work and when he attends he makes excuses to avoid going to meetings.

Patrick's Proposed Therapy

At the initial assessment the therapist explores Patrick's past and present functioning with him. He describes that ultimately, he would like to get married but worries he will not cope being the centre of attention on his wedding day. By the end of the initial assessment session the psychologist summarises some of the things they have spoken about and says:

"Thanks for your openness and honesty in our session today, I know that speaking about your feelings doesn't always come naturally. It seems that your experiences of the open plan office and glass walls reminded you of your secondary school where you were bullied about how you looked during your PE lessons. This caused you to become hyper aware of your thoughts and bodily sensations. It makes sense that you don't want to feel humiliated, and I think it would be helpful for us to work through what happened to you at school and help you to process how awful this was at the time. I would suggest that a mixture of cognitive behavioural therapy (CBT) and trauma work will help you be able to perform well at work again and to help all parts of you to fully appreciate that the bullying at school was in the past and that you're not at threat of this happening again currently."

Patrick's treatment outcomes

Patrick is seen for 14 sessions of psychological therapy. He responds well to the approach and is struck by how simply it seemed to get resolved but how awful it had been making him feel. He decides to undertake a mental health first aid training course so that he can optimally support any colleagues in future. He realises that before the therapy guilt, shame and trauma were holding him back. He plans to propose to his girlfriend when they go to Paris in the spring.

PART 3:

How to Do It

Why are you reaching out?

When researching therapists, it is important to consider why you are seeking talking therapy. A therapist may also want to know some of the answers to these questions when you meet, so it can be a good idea to have a little bit of a think about some of these areas.

❖ Is this your own decision or have you been advised to seek help?

❖ What model of therapy are you interested in? Sometimes someone has recommended a particular type of therapy to you but you don't know much about it. It's okay to discuss this with a potential therapist. You can also ask for their opinion of what therapy they think might be a good fit for you based on your current needs.

❖ What are your goals? For example, what would you like to be different?

❖ How will you know when you have reached your goals? How will change be tracked? A good therapist will discuss this with you, and it may include completing some questionnaires so that these changes can be tracked.

❖ How frequent would you like your sessions to be?

Titles and qualifications

It is important to understand the different titles used by therapists offering talking therapy.

Trust us, we know it's confusing. Sometimes titles are used to deliberately confuse too which makes it all the more befuddling.

The tricky bit is that some practitioners might well claim to be qualified in a certain field yet have only completed a basic course and in some circumstances have been found to have actually paid for a certificate in a certain type of therapy without completing the course. We have seen adverts from companies offering a course and certificate, for example in something like Cognitive Behavioural Therapy (CBT) for about the cost of a few cups of coffee. We can attest that this level of 'training' is entirely unsuitable to the magnitude of the actual training, skills and qualifications required to be able to practice safely, effectively and ethically. Insufficiently trained people might well lead to clients being unsafely treated which can place them at risk. If you'd like to know more about someone's training and qualifications, it's most definitely okay to ask.

Generally speaking, as a rule of thumb, qualifications obtained from actual bricks and mortar UK based universities are usually a more robust learning environment for the person being trained. We would consider the gold standard training to include some level of supervised practice whilst the student learns how to use the approach safely. Online courses which only require a few hours of passive watching of content are unlikely to offer the depth of knowledge, skills and experience that you deserve and need.

In the past, we have seen people claim to be qualified psychologists and even to claim that they have completed many, many more years' worth of work or training than they actually have in reality. Don't worry. We reported them to the Health and Care Professions Council (HCPC). The tricky bit is that because the terms 'psychologist', 'counsellor' and 'coach' are not protected terms that anyone, even someone who has never even picked up a book on mental health, can choose to brand themselves in this way.

Where to look up qualified and regulated individuals offering talking therapy

The Professional Standards Authority (PSA) accredited register is a huge step towards helping people find accredited and qualified practitioners working in this field, including psychologists, counsellors and psychotherapists. You can choose a profession, e.g. 'counsellor', 'practitioner psychologist', 'Psychiatrist' from the drop-down menu and it will provide links to the relevant professionally accredited registers for each group of practitioners. It advises you to:

'choose a practitioner who is on an accredited register'

https://www.professionalstandards.org.uk/home

Where people may advertise

There can be a variety of places where clinicians might advertise their services. Here are some examples:

❖ Personal or associate websites. Sometimes a clinician will only work for themselves but other times they might get some of their work from someone they pay a percentage of their fee to. This might explain why you see the same clinician advertising on a number of different company websites.

❖ Google adverts and ranked placements in search engine results.

❖ Paid therapy matching services such as Psychology Today and Counselling Directory. In order to appear in these sites, clinicians will pay a monthly fee of around £20. This then allows potential clients to navigate the site, read about different therapists and to find a good match based on location, therapy model and experience.

❖ An influencer or a friend may have recommended a clinician or service to you. It's worth bearing in mind that this still might not mean they will be the best fit of a clinician for you or that they are legitimately and appropriately qualified and experienced.

❖ Social Media sites, such as LinkedIn, allow people to list their qualifications and experiences. Please do bear in mind that these are formed by self-declaration and are not cross-referenced or corroborated by the universities or services they say they have been trained by.

To find qualified, regulated Psychologists

Once you think you have found someone you think might be a good fit for you, if they claim to be a qualified psychologist, it would be a good idea to check that they appear on the Health Care Professions Council (HCPC) register. The HCPC regulates all qualified practitioner Psychologists, art therapists and other professions such as paramedics, speech and language therapists, radiographers, dieticians and more offering services to the public.

https://www.hcpc-uk.org/

Whilst not a regulator, the British Psychological Society also provides a directory of Chartered psychologists offering services to the public. Do bear in mind that the BPS is an optional service therefore it is possible to be fully qualified and regulated but not choose to pay a fee to the BPS to be described as 'chartered'.

https://portal.bps.org.uk/Psychologist-Search/Directory-of-Chartered-Psychologists

Logos and memberships

Be aware that just because someone displays an impressive looking logo it doesn't necessarily mean that they are suitably qualified, accredited and/or regulated. Examples include using an accredited or professional logo yet not possessing the relevant qualification.

Always make sure you visit the website the logo refers to and look them up. Don't be tempted to take the logo alone as proof of qualification and regulation.

Health Care Professions council

T he logo below should only be professionally qualified people who are registered with the HCPC.

www.hcpc-uk.org

The BPS

On many occasions we have seen unqualified clinicians use, for example, a British Psychological Society (BPS) logo on their website or social media. There are a number of different BPS badges available for members to use – as a student, a graduate and as a chartered psychologist, to name a few.

It is possible to display a BPS logo when you have completed a 3-year undergraduate degree but this usually means you've received zero clinical skills training, just theory. It does not mean that person has completed any kind of professional (doctoral training) qualification or that they are necessarily deemed safe to be working with the general public.

The badge above which says chartered psychologist is one that people can display when they have completed a professional training programme as a qualified, or chartered, psychologist. They can then also use the letters 'CPsychol' after their name.[5]

It is worth bearing in mind that being a BPS member is not compulsory. It is also not free. It means that sometimes beautifully and appropriately qualified people will NOT choose

---

[5] Thanks to the organisations in this booklet for granting permission to share their logos with you in this section.

to register and pay to be a chartered member. However, there may be far less experienced and qualified people willing to pay for and display the *unqualified* graduate member badge which might imply they are more qualified than they actually are.

In Ireland

The Irish Association for Counsellors & Psychotherapy:

https://www.iacp.ie

Irish Psychologists:

https://www.psychologicalsociety.ie/footer/PSI-Chartered-Psychologist-Online-Directory

Evidence-based therapy

One of the key benefits of accessing qualified, regulated therapy is that it is more likely that your therapist has trained extensively whilst working with actual clients / patients rather than just learning about the theory. But of course, the theory is important too. In clinical practice we look at what is called 'the evidence-base' to help work out what is going to be the best fit of treatment for you as an individual based upon, your presenting problems, the things you have tried before alongside your needs, wishes and culture. In all of the example clients we met earlier, Angela, Fahra and Patrick, evidence-based approaches were used. The National Institute for Health and Care Excellence (NICE) work so hard on remaining up to date on which approaches have a robust evidence base. This guidance is commonly referred to as NICE guidance and covers a wide variety of clinical presentations where the results of the treatment are better than control groups and where the benefits of treatment outweigh any risks. If in doubt, ask your therapist what evidence base there is for the treatments they are proposing or using. It is okay to ask those questions.

Culturally Competent Therapy

A really important aspect of therapy is that it is culturally competent. This means that it meets the needs of your own culture and is up to date in terms of the current cultural context in which we live. It goes beyond simply having an awareness of these differences it means that an individual or organisation has the necessary skills, sensitivity and attitudes required to provide a service which enables clear effective communication and treatment whilst being ethical and respectful to individual and cultural beliefs and practices.

A culturally competent therapist or service will be aware and mindful of differences such as:

- Beliefs
- Customs
- Language
- Religious Beliefs
- Religious Practices

That said it is not always essential that a client is seen for therapy by a therapist who has the same personal or religious / cultural beliefs as themselves. In fact, many clients say that sometimes they purposefully choose someone with a different background to themselves so that they can develop an idea of how other cultures, practices and genders would respond to the difficulties they have so that they can adjust their own barometer for what equates to fair and equal treatment from others and to themselves. It is worth bearing in mind that some clinicians list their cultural competence in their adverts and in some cases you can use the search terms.

Clinic Addresses and Price Tags

Sometimes a particular clinic address or location can be used to imply that a service is better or that a higher cost is more justified because of the expensive location.

It's worth bearing in mind that it's a relatively easy process to rent therapy rooms and that this can even be done by the hour for a really low cost. For example, recently someone emailed[6] me offering me the chance to book therapy rooms located 'just off Harley Street' for £12 per hour.

Even when working from home, some clinicians may attempt to portray themselves as a premium service. Sometimes people will use photographs of exclusive and expensive buildings or therapy rooms on websites despite working from home and offering online only sessions.

Don't assume that because someone has a fancy location or charges a high price that their services are any better. You absolutely can pay a higher price if that's your choice. It is always appropriate to ask potential clinicians about their qualifications, registrations and level of experience.

---

[6] An unsolicited email which is also another unethical minefield!

Counsellors & Psychotherapists

Please note, in this section and the next we introduce you to the BACP and the BABCP. They have very similar acronyms but are different organisations.

For Counsellors and Psychotherapists, their professional registration is with the BACP (British Association of Counselling & Psychotherapy), or UKCP (United Kingdom Counsel for Psychotherapy). CBT therapists may be registered with the BACP but please also refer to the the next specific section for CBT Therapists.

https://www.bacp.co.uk

https://www.psychotherapy.org.uk

This is the logo you will see if someone is registered with the BACP.

CBT Therapists

CBT therapists are also registered with the BABCP (British Association for Behavioural and Cognitive Psychotherapies).

https://babcp.com/CBTRegister/Search#/

It is important to familiarise yourself with the Accreditation process for the BABCP as CBT Therapists may be qualified but still working towards their accreditation. This means that they are able to conduct CBT sessions but are still working towards the next level of accreditation.

The BABCP is the lead organisation for cognitive and behavioural therapies in the UK and Ireland. They provide practitioner accreditation for CBT Therapists living and working in the UK and Ireland.

Accreditation means that a CBT Therapist has both core professional mental health training, or a recognised equivalent, as well as specific CBT training. To be accredited, members must have applied and demonstrated that they meet high standards of training and experience in CBT.

More information on this is explained here:

https://babcp.com/Accreditation/What-is-Accreditation

Remember, there is also an organisation to check the professional standards for CBT practitioners. It is called The Professional Standards Agency (PSA). It is an accredited register and is a huge step towards helping people find accredited and qualified practitioners working in this field.

https://www.professionalstandards.org.uk/what-we-do/accredited-registers/find-a-register

This is the logo you will see if someone is registered with the BABCP.

Eye Movement Desensitisation and Reprocessing (EMDR)

Practitioners offering Eye Movement Desensitisation Therapy (EMDR) to the public need to have conducted an approved course and be accredited with **EMDR UK** and Europe.

Register
https://emdrassociation.org.uk/find-a-therapist/

The following information is cited on their website:

"All therapists listed on this site are accredited with **EMDR UK** and Europe. This means they have proven levels of experience and competency in **EMDR** therapy beyond the foundation training, and have to prove that they are continuing to keep their skills up to date. There are three categories of accredited therapist as follows:

Practitioners are therapists who have been supervised in their **EMDR** practice beyond the foundation training and demonstrated their competence to an **EMDR** Consultant.

Consultants are therapists who have demonstrated higher levels of experience and competency, including supervising and accrediting other **EMDR** therapists.

Trainers are highly experienced **EMDR** therapists who have undertaken a rigorous programme of development and study. They train other therapists in **EMDR** therapy and have demonstrated competence to a governing committee of the Europe Board.

You may find your therapist is not listed on this site. This could be because they have completed an accredited foundation training but are not accredited with EMDR Europe. Please check their accredited training certificate and that their core mental health profession is being maintained. It could be that your therapist did not complete an accredited training. We would not recommend you seek EMDR therapy from these clinicians. EMDR is an advanced psychotherapy requiring a high level of skill. Unaccredited courses will not give the therapist confidence or competence in this approach and could leave you at risk. See "EMDR Association" website.

Awkward, what if I don't like my therapist?

However old you are currently, you have likely met people so far that you just don't like. Whilst we hope this isn't the case for a therapist you begin working with it's not impossible. We hope this might be less common in private practice where you will likely have a freer choice over choosing your therapist but even then, sometimes a client decides they have chosen wrong.

The "fit" between therapist and client is important. We like to think of fit in 2 parts: the right clinical/training background and also the fit between you as two individuals. You can have a therapist who has the right skills and experience yet there is not the right feeling between you when you work together. This may be awkward, but it is absolutely ok to address this between you. We both routinely ask our clients whether the fit is working between us. It is a routine part of our work. So, please, if you feel able, talk to your therapist about this before withdrawing. This is because sometimes trying to draw therapy to a close can be a part of repeating patterns from the past which may not always have served your best interests.

However, if you just don't like the way you are being treated or don't like them it is okay to make a different choice and to end your current therapeutic relationship. If you have followed the advice, we have offered so far but you have some concerns about the ethics or professionalism of the qualified, regulated therapist you have been working with you can contact their relevant regulatory body as detailed earlier in this booklet. Your concerns will be taken seriously, and you will usually be kept up to date with any action and steps taken.

PART 4:

Additional useful information & checklists

Sourcing a therapist summary

So, now you know what all the terms and considerations are, where does this leave you when sourcing a therapist? While this is not an exhaustive or definitive list, we have attempted to document some important things for you to consider.

Let's take a quick look at the key pointers and guidance we have covered in this booklet.

1. What qualifications do they claim to have? Feel free to **ASK** for this information and look them up.
2. An appropriately qualified and regulated practitioner will have absolutely no issue with this and will in fact encourage you to do so.
3. A red flag may be those who are reluctant or evasive around sharing or discussing their training and qualifications.
4. Are they registered with a professional body outlined on the Professional Standards Agency (PSA) accredited register or, for Psychologists, the HCPC register?
3. Are they registered with the Information Commissioner's Office (ICO) for the purposes of data collection, storage and handling? Their role is to uphold information rights in the best interests of the public.
4. If you are using Health Insurance to pay for your therapy, then these companies also employ rigorous checks on the practitioners they use and will provide you with a list of approved practitioners.

5. If you are paying privately, then fees will vary between different types of practitioner. However, the fees should be clearly stated and payment terms clear. It is a contractual agreement.
6. Regulators such as the **HCPC** and **BACP** have information on their websites about what the public should expect from the professional they are working with.

Summary "Questions for you" pointers

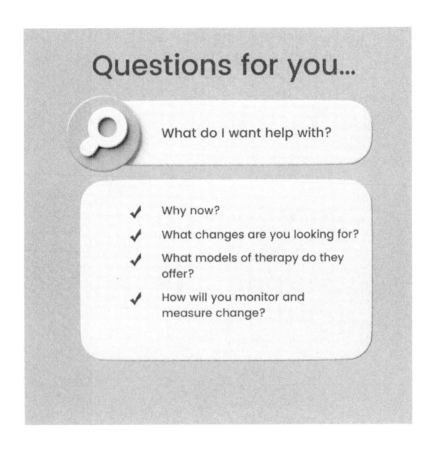

Questions for you...

The therapist I am thinking of...

- ✔ What qualifications do they have?
- ✔ Are they qualified in what they claim to be offering?
- ✔ Do they have a professional regulator?
- ✔ Have you looked them up on the regulator directory?

Questions for you...

The Therapist I am thinking of continued.....

✔ Do they have professional indemnity insurance?

✔ Are they registered with the ICO? (Information Commissioner's Office)

✔ Are there any red flags showing up?

Questions for you...

Logistics

- ✔ What are their charges and are they clearly outlined?
- ✔ What are their payment methods?
- ✔ What are their terms and conditions?
- ✔ When and where do they work?
- ✔ Is it accessible for your needs?

Questions for you...

 Logistics continued....

✔ For online sessions- do you
   have somewhere private to
   talk?

✔ What do you have before and
   after your session?

✔ Can you create time for
   yourself after your
   sessions?

Index

Printed in Great Britain
by Amazon

36896158R00046